Family Means Love

Dr. Andrew Vassall
Unc Jon

Praise for Family Means Love

"Family Means Love reminds us that the definition of family is those who love you, and being part of a family is special."

LISE MARLOWE - TEACHER

"Family Means Love should be on every teacher's and library's bookshelf. It beautifully illustrates diverse families so every child can see their own family affirmed and included."

ANDREW ALTMAN - TEACHER

"What a wonderful story! As a School Counselor, I really appreciate the diverse representation of families. I think all of my students could find a familiar portrayal of love in this book. I'm excited to share this with my students!"

CHRIS SOLEIL - SCHOOL COUNSELOR

"Family Means Love is a simple, elegant story that describes the love experienced in all types of families today. I appreciate the recognition of many types of families beyond the traditional nuclear family."

DAYNA GILLIARD - PARENT

Families can be big or small,

Love can be shown in many ways,

But time spent with family is the best love of all.

This dream could not have been possible without the support of God, and my family units.

A special shout out to all my students, thank you for your inspiration.

I know my step-mom loves me...

Because she always reads stories to me.

We are a family.

I know my older sister loves me...
Because she plays dress up with
me and takes our picture.

We are a family.

I know my mom and dad love me...

Because they take turns taking me

to school in the morning.

We are a family.

I know my grandparents love me...

Because even though they live far away

they always wish me a happy birthday.

We are a family.

I know my dad loves me...

Because when he comes to visit he always takes me to play in the park.

We are a family.

I know my mom loves me...
Because she takes care of me all by herself and teaches me how to cook my favorite food.

We are a family.

I know my grandparents love me...

Because they take care of me and

we go for walks on the beach together.

We are a family.

I know my mom loves me...

Because when we spend weekends together she lets me help in her garden.

We are a family.

I know my dads love me...

Because they always cheer me on

at my baseball games.

We are a family.

I know my older brother loves me...

Because he takes care of me all by himself

and always makes chores fun.

We are a family.

I know my step-dad loves me...

Because he always teaches me how

to do new things.

We are a family.

I know my aunt and uncle love me...

Because they spoil me and

take me to museums.

We are a family.

I know my mom and dad who
are not married love me...
Because they always make me
feel better when I am sick.
We are a family.

I know my younger brother loves me...

Because he always copies whatever I do.

We are a family.

I know my dad loves me...
Because he takes care of me all by himself and always tells jokes to make me laugh.

We are a family.

I know my two moms love me...

Because we always have fun playing games together.

We are a family.

I know my step-brother loves me...

Because he always lets me

play video games with him.

We are a family.

I know my grandfather loves me...

Because he lives with me

and we sing and dance together.

We are a family.

I know my family loves me...

Because they tell me "I love you!"

Questions

1. What was the story about?

2. How did the story make you feel?

3. The_____family reminds me of my family.

4. My_____loves me because _____.

Copyright © 2021 Andrew Vassall

ISBN #978-1-7372324-5-2 PBK
ISBN #978-1-7372324-6-9 EBK
ISBN #978-1-7372324-7-6 ABK

April 2022

Published and Distributed by
Dr. Vassall's Literacy Tree

ALL RIGHTS RESERVED. No part of this book publication may be reproduced, stored in a retrieval system, or transmitted in any form or by any means- electronic, mechanical, photo-copy, recording, or any other-except brief quotation in reviews, without the prior permission of the author or publisher.

Made in the USA
Middletown, DE
09 July 2022

68893667R00027